SUGGESTIONS

FOR THE FORMATION OF A

MEDICAL MISSIONARY SOCIETY,

OFFERED TO THE

CONSIDERATION OF ALL CHRISTIAN NATIONS,

MORE ESPECIALLY

TO THE KINDRED NATIONS OF

ENGLAND AND THE UNITED STATES OF AMERICA.

Canton, China:
OCTOBER, 1836.

SUGGESTIONS.

Viewing with peculiar interest the good effects that seem likely to be produced by medical practice among the Chinese, especially as tending to bring about a more social and friendly intercourse between them and foreigners, as well as to diffuse the arts and sciences of Europe and America, and in the end introduce the gospel of our Savior in place of the pitiable superstitions by which their minds are now governed, we have resolved to attempt the foundation of a society to be called the "Medical Missionary Society in China."

The objects we have in view in the foundation of a Society of this description are:

1st, That those who shall come out as medical missionaries to China may find here those to whom they can apply for assistance and information, on their first arrival in the country.

2d, That by this means their services may be made immediately available, while, at the same time, they may be put in the way of learning the language for the purpose of fitting themselves to practice in parts of the country to which foreigners have not hitherto gained free access.

3d, We do not propose to *appoint* individuals to the work, but to receive and assist the medical men who shall be sent out by Societies formed for the purpose either in England or America. Being acquainted with the peculiarities of the case, our especial desire is to draw attention to the selection of men of suitable qualifications.

4th, We therefore propose to receive any sums of money which may be given in aid of this object, and to disburse them as shall be deemed expedient, until *the Society* be formed, so that the labors of those who engage in the cause shall not be retarded.

Individuals, subscribing fifty dollars, or upwards, in one payment, shall be considered members for life; or fifteen dollars annually, members during the period of their subscriptions.

In further illustration of our views we would here premise, that in order to the success of the object contemplated, those who engage in it must not receive any pecuniary *remuneration:* the work throughout must be, and appear to be, one of *disinterested benevolence.* It is indispensable that the men who shall conduct the institution be not only masters of their profession, and conciliating in their manners towards all classes, but *judicious* men—men thoroughly imbued with the spirit of *genuine piety*, ready to endure hardships, and to sacrifice personal comfort, that they may commend the gospel of our Lord and Savior, and so coöperate in its introduction among the millions of this partially civilized yet '*mysterious*' and idolatrous empire—men willing to suffer the loss of all things for joys that await those who *for Christ's sake* do good on earth.

In addition to the *Ophthalmic Hospital* already established, other departments are equally needed, and each would fully occupy the time and talents of one medical person. Among these may be mentioned,

A Surgical department, for the treatment of cases requiring the interposition of the surgeon, as the removal of tumors, cure of ulcers, reduction of fractured and dislocated limbs, and the like.

A Department for the ear. A vast amount of good may be effected by curing the affections of this organ, which perhaps are as numerous as those of the eyes, or even more so. The man who shall publish a treatise in Chinese, accompanied by a statement of facts, that shall correct the pernicious practice of barbers who introduce a sharp cutting instrument into the ear, by which violence is frequently done to this delicate organ, will deserve well of the Chinese nation, for it is a national evil.

A Department for cutaneous affections. In no country in the world, are diseases of this class more numerous and aggravated; and added to the misfortune of being thus afflicted, if the disease of the sufferer is *suspected* to be malignant and contagious, he is liable to be deprived of his liberty, and immured during the remainder of life.

A Department for diseases of females. Daily experience has disclosed that these are very numerous, and in some instances exceedingly aggravated, and but little understood by Chinese physicians. And contrary to expectation, facts have demonstrated that the seclusion, characteristic of the upper classes of Chinese females, does not restrain them from applying to foreign practitioners with the hope of relief from these calamities.

A Department for the diseases of children. An inconceivable amount of suffering is endured by children in China, which in many instances might be avoided, but for the ignorance of parents and want of medical aid and advice. The merchants from distant provinces, who trade at Canton, are often attended by members of their families, and frequently have brought their children for medical treatment. We cannot suppose the fond parent will remain insensible to the obligations of gratitude when he returns to his own home, or fail to speak there of the *excluded foreigner* who had gratuitously restored his child to the blessings of health... We conceive there cannot be a more direct avenue to influence than will be presented in this department, and the impression may be far more enduring than that made in almost any other way ; for while in the case of the aged, who receive medicine from the foreigner, the remembrance may quickly depart with them ; it may be otherwise in respect to the babe and the youth, who are, by the hand of charity, rescued from a premature grave, or from diseases which uncontrolled might extend through life.

Regarding it desirable that these several departments be established as soon as Providence shall prepare the way, and the men and means are provided, we would also recommend to Societies, while they are sending out medical persons, not to neglect to encourage pious and well-disposed young men to accompany them, with a view to becoming dressers and apothecaries, and to render themselves useful in the supervision of the internal concerns of the hospitals.

Here it may be proper to repeat, and with the utmost emphasis, that all who engage in this work should be JUDICIOUS *men, thoroughly imbued with the spirit of* TRUE PIETY, *willing to endure hardships and to sacrifice personal comforts.*

We cannot close these suggestions without adverting to one idea, though this is not the place to enlarge upon it. It is affecting to contemplate this empire, embracing three hundred and sixty millions of souls, where almost all the light of true science is unknown, where Christianity has *scarcely* shed one genial ray, and where the theories concerning matter and mind, creation and providence, are wofully destitute of truth; it is deeply affecting to see the multitudes who are here suffering under maladies, from which the hand of charity is able to relieve them.

Now we know indeed that it is the 'glorious gospel of the blessed God' only that can set free the human mind, and that it is only when enlightened in the true knowledge of God that man is rendered capable of rising to his true intellectual elevation; but while we take care to give this truth the high place which it ought ever to hold, we should beware of depreciating other truth. All truth is of God; the introduction of medical truth into China would be the demolition of much error.

In the vast conflict which is to revolutionize the intellectual and moral world we may not underrate the value of any weapon. As a means then to waken the dormant mind of China, may we not place a high value upon medical truth, and seek its introduction with good hope of its becoming the handmaid of religious truth? If an inquiry after truth upon any

subject is elicited, is there not a great point gained ?
And that inquiry after medical truth may be provoked,
there is good reason to expect : for, exclusive as China is, in all her systems, she cannot exclude disease,
nor shut her people up from the desire of relief. Does
not then the finger of Providence point clearly to one
way that we should take with the people of China,
directing us to seek the introduction of the remedies
for sin itself, by the same door through which we convey those which are designed to mitigate or remove
its evils ?

Although medical truth cannot restore the sick and
afflicted to the favor of God ; yet perchance, the spirit
of inquiry about it, once awakened, will not sleep till
it inquires after the Source of truth ; and he who
comes with the blessings of health may prove an angel
of mercy to point to the Lamb of God.

At any rate, this seems the only open door ; let us
enter it. Loathsome disease in every hopeless form,
has uttered her cry for relief from every corner of the
land ; we have heard it, and would and must essay
its healing. A faith that worketh not may wait for
other doors. None can deny that *this* is a way of
charity that worketh no ill, and our duty to walk in it
seems plain and imperative.

We most confidently rely on the aid of the pious
and benevolent in the accomplishment of this great

work, and when the millions which compose this mighty empire shall feel the influence of true religion and civilization, when the light of Christianity shall take the place of the dark cloud of Paganism, which now envelopes them, then will be fulfilled, in its spiritual sense, the prophecy of Isaiah : "The eyes of the blind shall be opened, and the ears of the deaf shall be unstopped; the lame shall leap as an hart, and the tongue of the dumb sing."

THOMAS R. COLLEDGE,
PETER PARKER,
E. C. BRIDGMAN.

China, October 5th, 1836.

APPENDIX.

A FRIEND, who is particularly interested in the subject of the foregoing pages, has expressed a wish that a brief statement of what has been already accomplished in China, by medical practice, might be added here by way of appendix. If full statements respecting the introduction of vaccination among the Chinese, the opening and successful conducting of the Ophthalmic Hospital at Macao, as well as of the one more recently established in Canton, were not before the public, such an appendix would be very desirable. But the feasibility and utility of medical practice by foreigners among the Chinese, are now so evident that a republication of former statements seems unnecessary. However, a reference to those documents with some extracts from the last Report of the hospital in Canton, may be appended.

The practice of vaccination was first introduced among the Chinese in the year 1805, by Alexander Pearson, esq., then surgeon to the Honorable East India Company's factory in Canton. Before that gentleman left China in the autumn of 1832, he had the satisfaction of knowing that the practice was not only well established in Canton, where it had been conducted under his own supervision, but that it had spread to nearly all the provinces of the empire. For a detailed account of this subject, from Mr. Pearson's own pen, see Chinese Repository, vol. ii, p. 36-41, for May, 1833.

The Ophthalmic Hospital in Macao was opened in 1827, and continued in successful operation till 1832, when the increased amount of practice among his own countrymen and other foreigners, occasioned by Dr. Pearson's return to England, compelled its founder to close its doors. In 1834, a brief account of the hospital was published in Canton by a 'philanthropist.' Some notices of it also appeared in the Chinese Repository: see vol. ii, p. 270; vol. iii, p. 364. By a reference to those several papers it will be seen that more than *four thousand* indigent and diseased Chinese were relieved from various maladies, and many restored to sight.

The hospital in Canton was opened on the 4th of November, 1835. The whole number of patients up to August, 1836, was 1674. For detailed accounts of the institution, during its first and second quarters, see Chinese Repository, vol. iv, p. 461; vol. v, p. 32.

The following is the list of diseases presented at the Ophthalmic Hospital in Canton, from the 4th of November, 1835, to the 4th of August, 1836. 1st, of the eye, 2d, miscellaneous.

1st:		
Amaurosis	- -	85
Acute ophthalmia	-	138
Chronic ophthalmia	-	71
Purulent ophthalmia	-	52
Scrofulous ophthalmia		6
Rheumatic ophthalmia		16
Ophthalmitis	- -	2
Ophthalmia tarsi	-	18
Ophthalmia variola	-	28
Conjunctivitis	- -	25
Hordeolum	- -	26
Cataract	- -	103
Entropia	- -	135
Ectropia	- -	2
Trichiasis	- -	35
Pterygium	- -	62
Opacity and vascularity of the cornea	-	263
Ulceration of the cornea		61
Nebula	- -	68
Albugo	- -	84
Leucoma	- -	28

Adipose thickening of the cornea	- -	14
Staphyloma	- -	74
Staphyloma sclerotica		7
Onyx	- -	10
Iritis	- -	35
Lippitudo	- -	15
Night blindness	-	9
Day blindness	-	2
Synechia anterior	-	29
Synechia posterior	-	14
Myosis	- -	15
Closed pupil with deposition of coagulable lymph		21
Procidentia iridis	-	7
Glaucoma	- -	7
Exophthalmia	- -	4
False vision	- -	2
Atrophy	- -	49
Hypertrophy	- -	9
Complete loss of one eye		20
Loss of both eyes	-	92

Mucocele - -	1
Muscæ volitantes -	2
Malignant ulcer of the upper lid - . -	1
Encysted tumor of the upper lid - -	1
Tumor from the external angle of the right eye, causing it to protrude upwards, out of its orbit	1
Injuries of the eye -	5
Sclerotitis - -	2
Choroiditis - -	2
Hydrops oculi - -	3
Tumors of the eyelids	2
Paralysis of the muscles of the lid - -	3
Quivering lid - -	1
Obstruction of the nasal duct - - -	2
Tumors from the conjunc- tiva - - -	5
Weak eyes - -	7
Adhesion of the conjunc- tiva to the cornea -	2
Preternatural growth from the lower portion of the orbit and near the external angle of the right eye, resembling a congeries of veins	1
Disease of the caruncula lachrymalis - -	1
2d: Abscess of the parotid gland - - -	2
Abscess of the arm -	1
Abscess of the hand -	2
Abscess of the thigh -	1
Abscess of the ear -	8
Abscess of the head -	2
Abscess of the face -	4
Abscess psoas - -	2
Cancer of the face -	1
Disease of lower jaw -	5
Luxation of the lower jaw	1
Necrosis of the lower jaw	2

Hydrocephalus - - ,	1
Disease of the antrum maxillare - -	1
Benign polypus of the nose	5
Malignant polypus of the nose - - -	1
Ranulæ - - -	2
Enlarged tonsils -	2
Polypus of the ear -	1
Deficiency of cerumen	4
Deposition of cerumen	5
Imperforate auditory fora- men - - -	2
Enlargement of meatus	2
Deafness - - -	7
Deafness with enlargement of the bones of the ear	2
Deaf and dumb child-	1
Dumbness - -	3
Anasarca - -	6
Ascites - - -	1
Dropsy - - -	4
Ovarian dropsy - -	2
Hydatids of the uterus	1
Cauliflower excrescence of uterus - - -	1
Amenorrhœa -	2
Chronic cystitis -	1
Cancer of the breast -	4
Goitre - - -	2
Scrofula - - -	3
Asthma - - -	2
Bronchitis -	1
Bronchial flux - -	1
Croup - - -	1
Sarcomatous tumor -	11
Encysted tumor -	3
Abdominal tumor -	3
Hernia direct - -	2
Hernia inguinal -	3
Curvature of the spine -	3
Curvature of the spine with paralysis -	4
Paraphlegia - -	1
Paralysis of the arm -	1
Phymosis, natural -	3

Hydrops articuli	-	3	
Acne	-	3	
Herpes	-	4	
Ichthyosis	-	2	
Psoriasis	-	1	
Tinea capitis	-	2	
Impetigo	-	3	
Intermittent fever	-	2	
Dyspepsia	-	2	
Indolent ulcer of the foot with elephantiasis	-	1	

Urinary calculus (removed) - - - 1

Needle by accident thrust into the breast, just below the sternum - 1

Needle, thrust into the palm of a child's hand, removed by a magnet, after an incision with a lancet, a month subsequent to the accident. 1

The two following cases, selected from the last quarterly Report, will serve as specimens of those which have been treated in Canton and at Macao: the remarks and ode, by Ma szeyay, will likewise afford an example of many similar tokens of respect and gratitude, which have been exhibited by the inmates of the hospitals.

———

No. 1283. Fungus Hæmatodes of the eye. Yat Akwang, of the district of Pwanyu, aged 4 years, entered the hospital May 4th, and remained a few days under medical treatment. The disease commenced about four months before, between the sclerotica and conjunctiva of the upper lid, and gradually increased till the whole eye was concealed. When the child came to the hospital, a large protruding ulcer appeared in the situation of the left eye, and the least irritation caused it to bleed. The child inclined his head to the opposite side, and was very feeble. The father was told that it could not then be removed, but he might return on the first of June, and if circumstances justified, I would extirpate it. Early in June he returned. The diseased mass had grown rapidly, and the protruded eye which came down upon the cheek as low as the mouth, was six or seven inches in circumference. The fate of the child, if the tumor was left to itself, was evident. The father wished it removed, and, being told the measure might prove fatal, said it was better for his child to die than live in such a condition. The possibility of its returning, should the operation not prove unsuccessful, being also explained, he still desired it to be performed. On the 26th, the eye was extirpated. From the history of the case, it was possible the eye itself might be sound, but covered with a fungus. I proceeded with the operation accordingly, but soon found the whole was diseased. Without much difficulty the eye was detached from the surrounding parts, and the optic nerve divided below the globe of the eye. The little child endured the operation with much fortitude. The hemorrhage was not great. But little inflammation succeeded, yet on the third day after, fears were entertained for the life of the child; but on the 9th day, the wound had quite healed, and the lids fell in and the child's appetite returned, and his prospects were flattering. However, the appearance of the optic nerve at its section being diseased, and presenting in its centre a dry yellow substance, like the cerumen of the ear, rendered the result suspicious. Before leaving, the little boy had become robust and playful. He has since returned, and to my deep regret the relief afforded him is to be momentary. The fungus has returned and attained half its former size, and that in less than three months from its removal.

No. 446. The case of Akae is mentioned in the first report, under date of December 27th, 1835. About three months subsequent to the removal of the original tumor, as she was walking by the river side, a coolie, carelessly passing by, thrust the end of the bamboo, with which he carried his burden, against the superciliary ridge of the right temple, from which the tumor had been removed. When she came to the hospital about a month after the accident, there was considerable tumefaction above the eye. It being the close of that term, she was directed to remain at home until the first of June; at which time the tumor had attained the magnitude of the former one, though not exactly the same shape, and others previously on the side of her face were enlarged. The new one was altogether of a different character from the former. It had the appearance of a spongy mass, and was bounded on the left by an exostosis from the superciliary process one eighth of an inch deep, and one inch and a half long at its base, forming an irregular perpendicular ridge; the tumor grew rapidly and was fast tending to suppuration; the general health was affected, and death seemed probable and that speedily, unless its progress could be arrested by a surgical operation, while the heat of midsummer not a little increased the hazard of such a measure. After repeated consultations with Dr. Cox and Mr. Jardine, who had assisted in the former instance, it was resolved to embrace the first favorable day for the operation. On the 21st of July, the operation was performed. On the first incision being made, a large quantity of greenish fluid gushed out from cells of disorganized matter. Two eliptical incisions from the middle of the forehead down the cheek to a level with the ear were first made, and then a third from the middle of the first incision back upon the side of the head to a point five inches above the ear. The whole cyst was completely dissected out upon the temple, and even portions of the pericranium were removed, showing distinctly the bloody appearance of the cranium caused by the contusion of the bamboo. The tumors above the ear were all removed, and what on the former occasion was supposed to be the parotid gland and its accessory gland, were sarcomatous tumors, occupying their situations; these were also removed, together with a tumor lying deep in the temporal fossa. There was a loss of about sixteen ounces of blood. The extreme warmth of the weather rendering it necessary to dress the wound daily, on the following day there was found considerable tumefaction above the eye, which finally suppurated. The incisions for the most part healed in the same kind manner as before, and but for the suppuration that took place beneath the integuments, would have healed with the same rapidity. The exostosis has not advanced beyond what it was at the operation. The constitution suffered much more than in the former instance, but she has very much regained her strength and the flesh she had lost, and now looks forward to the prospect of returning home in a few days, with the hope of enjoying a happy reprieve from the grave.

I will conclude this brief report by subjoining a translation of some lines written by Ma szeay (in the first report called *Matszeah*), the private secretary to the chefoo, as they will serve to illustrate the ideas and feelings which he and other patients entertain respecting the hospital. The translation is by Mr. Morrison, to whose kindness I am under many obligations. It has been put into verse by a friend. The stiffness of the style is a necessary consequence of faithfulness to the original. The old gentleman's gratitude has ever seemed unfeigned, and when dismissed from the hospital, he requested leave to send a painter and take " my likeness that he might bow down before it every day." He had previously intimated his intention of writing an ode. The painting was refused. The ode, preceded by a few explanatory remarks by Ma szeay is as follows.

Doctor Parker is a native of America, one of the nations of the western ocean. He is of a good and wealthy family, loves virtue, and takes pleasure in distributing to the necessities of others: he is moreover very skillful in the medical art. In the ninth month of the year *Yihwe*, he crossed the seas, and came to Canton, where he opened an institution in which to exercise gratuitously his medical talents. Hundreds of patients daily sought relief from his hands. Sparing neither expense nor toil, from morning to evening, he exercised the tenderest compassion towards the sick and miserable.

I had then lost the sight of my left eye, seven years, and the right eye had sympathized with it nearly half that period. No means used proved beneficial ; no physician had been able to bring me relief. In the eleventh month of the year above named, my friend Muh Keaeshaou introduced me to doctor Parker, by whom I was directed to convey my bedding to his hospital. I there made my dormitory in a third story, where he visited me night and morning. First he administered a medicine in powder, the effects of which, as a cathartic, continued three days. He then performed an operation on the eye with a silver needle, after which he closed up the eye with a piece of cloth. In five days, when this was removed, a few rays of light found entrance, and in ten-days I was able to distinguish perfectly. He then operated on the right eye, in like manner. I had been with him nearly a month when, the year drawing to a close, business compelled me to take leave. On leaving, I wished to present an offering of thanks; but he peremptorily refused it, saying, "return, and give thanks to heaven and earth: what merit have I?" So devoid was he of boasting. Compare this his conduct, with that of many physicians of celebrity. How often do they demand heavy fees, and dose you for months together, and after all fail to benefit. Or how often, if they afford even a partial benefit, do they trumpet forth their own merits, and demand costly acknowledgments! But this doctor, heals men at his own cost, and though perfectly successful, ascribes all to heaven, and absolutely refuses to receive any acknowledgment. How far beyond those of the common order of physicians are his character and rank! Ah, such men are difficult to find. The following hasty lines I have penned, and dedicate them to him.

A fluid, darksome and opaque, long time had dimmed my sight,
For seven revolving weary years one eye was lost to light;
The other, darkened by a film, during three years saw no day,   [ray.
High heaven's bright and gladd'ning light could not pierce it with its

Long, long, I sought the hoped relief, but still I sought in vain,
My treasures, lavished in the search, bought no relief from pain;
Till, at length, I thought my garments I must either pawn or sell,
And plenty in my house I feared was never more to dwell.

Then loudly did I ask, for what cause such pain I bore,—
For transgressions in a former life unatoned for before?
But again came the reflection, how, of yore, oft, men of worth,
For slight errors had borne suff'ring great as drew my sorrow forth.

" And shall not one," said I then, " whose worth is but as nought,
" Bear patiently, as heaven's gift, what it ordains!" The thought
Was scarce completely formed, when of a friend the footstep fell
On my threshold, and I breathed a hope he had words of joy to tell.

" I have heard," the friend who enter'd said, "there is come to us of late'
" A native of the ' flower'd flag's' far off and foreign state;
" O'er tens of thousand miles of sea to the inner land he's come;
" His hope and aim to heal men's pain, he leaves his native home."

I quick went forth, this man I sought, this gen'rous doctor found;
He gained my heart, he's kind and good; for, high up from the ground,
He gave a room, to which he came, at morn, at eve, at night,—
Words were but vain were I to try his kindness to recite.

With needle argentine, he pierced the cradle of the tear;
What fears I felt! Soo Tungpo's words rung threat'ning in my ear:
" Glass hung in mist," the poet says, "take heed you do not shake;"
(The words of fear rung in my ear) "how if it chance to break."

The fragile lens his needle pierced: the dread, the sting, the pain,
I thought on these, and that the cup of sorrow I must drain:
But then my mem'ry faithful showed the work of fell disease,
How long the orbs of sight were dark, and I deprived of ease.

And thus I thought: if now, indeed, I were to find relief:
' Twere not too much to bear the pain, to bear the present grief.
Then the words of kindness, which I heard, sunk deep into my soul,
And free from fear I gave myself to the foreigner's control.

His silver needle sought the lens, and quickly from it drew
The opaque and darksome fluid, whose effects so well I knew ;
His golden probe soon clear'd the lens, and then my eyes he bound,
And lav'd with water, sweet as is the dew to thirsty ground.

Three days thus lay I, prostrate, still; no food then could I eat,
My limbs relax'd were stretch'd as though th' approach of death to meet;
With thoughts astray—mind ill at ease—away from home and wife,
I often thought that by a thread was hung my precious life.

Three days I lay, no food had I, and nothing did I feel ;
Nor hunger, sorrow, pain, nor hope, nor thought of woe or weal ;
My vigor fled, my life seemed gone, when, sudden, in my pain,
There came one ray — one glimmering ray, I see,—I live again !

As starts from visions of the night, he who dreams a fearful dream,
As from the tomb, uprushing comes, one restored to day's bright beam,
Thus, I with gladness and surprise, with joy, with keen delight,
See friends and kindred crowd around, I hail the blessed light :

With grateful heart, with heaving breast, with feelings flowing o'er,
I cried, " O lead me quick to him who can the sight restore !"
To kneel I tried, but he forbade ; and, forcing me to rise,
" To mortal man bend not the knee;" then pointing to the skies:—

" I 'm but," said he, " the workman's tool, another's is the hand ;
" Before his might, and in his sight, men, feeble, helpless, stand :
" Go, virtue learn to cultivate, and never thou forget
" That, for some work of future good thy life is spared thee yet !"

The off'ring, token of my thanks, he refused ; nor would he take
Silver or gold, they seemed as dust ; 'tis but for virtue's sake
His works are done.   His skill divine I ever must adore,
Nor lose remembrance of his name till life's last day is o'er.

Thus have I told, in these brief words, this learned doctor's praise,
Well does his worth deserve that I should tablets to him raise.—

[What he says, of my calling on him to give thanks to earth, of my rich
family, &c., is to be received with due allowance as Chinese embellishment.]

CPSIA information can be obtained
at www.ICGtesting.com
Printed in the USA
LVHW061340200623
750141LV00004B/257